UNMASK

Lyndsy Flanagan

I want to dedicate this book to my grandma, Helen.
She taught me by example how to be vulnerable and how to overcome. She would pray for me, write me letters, and plead with me to serve God in my darkest days.
She would play Joyce Meyer as loud as she could, hoping I would listen to her words. She's been my absolute biggest supporter in writing and in my ministry.

Grandma, I love you dearly!

TABLE OF CONTENTS

FOREWARD

I n this book Lyndsy opens her heart and life to the reader.

She skillfully shares her story with amazing insight that will minister to everyone who has walked through rejection and spent their life searching for answers and healing.

UNMASKED is full of wisdom born out of experience. A wonderful tool and resource that can be used individually or to minister to many hurting from the wound of rejection and help them come to understand the scripture..." Ye shall know the Truth and the Truth shall make you free." John 8:32.

–Bishop Anne Gimenez

Humility, honesty, transparency, and vulnerability are essential to the process of unmasking. But why is this process so difficult to walk out? None of us want to live in pain. Could it be that fear of rejec- tion and abandonment from those we want accep- tance from causes us to keep the Mask on?

Lyndsy Flanagan understands this journey unlike no other. Her INCREDIBLE and AMAZING book "Unmask" provides a highway of healing and hope, that Lyndsy has personally traveled and, as a result is a living testimony of the MIRACLE revealed by saying yes to being Unmasked.

As you give yourself to the information and the impartation that awaits you, may every word you read release you from shame, affirm your God given identity, and remind you that the beauty behind the Mask is so worth fighting for!!

–Eddie James

ACKNOWLEDGEMENTS

This story has been nothing short of hard for me to put on paper. I never thought I would go back and take my most vulnerable moments and put them in a book for everyone to see but I knew it was part of my destiny.

I feel this book is a step of obedience. It's been a journey, to say the least – of fear, selfdoubt, and fear of resurfacing the harder times in my life but I am constantly reminded of the women who went before me who shared their stories so bravely that kept me going.

The most life-changing moments I have had in my journey with the Lord has been raw and unfiltered conversations with other women, leaving me to realize we are all on the road to find who it is that God designed us to be just one layer at a time.

I want to thank all the women who have ever been a part of Unmask in any capacity for believing in this message of uncovering your identity through vulnerability.

Thank you to the ladies of Unmask who sat with me, cried with me, and began to transform their cities by being vulnerable and brave enough to share their stories of beauty from ashes. This includes my hometown girls in Warren and Youngstown; you all share a very special place in my heart.

Thank you to the ladies who stepped up and started chapters of Unmask in their cities when I truly had no idea what I was doing but lived in faith with me as we brought this vision to life.

I want to thank my family for supporting me and believing in me. My mom – who is my rock – my step dad who reads my blogs and has listened to me throughout the stress of writing this story. My sister, who continues to remind me who I am when I tend to be my worst critic; you're my best friend in the entire world. My dad, who has believed in me and pushed me to fulfill my dreams.

My brother, who has been a walking miracle and a testament to the goodness of God.

My husband for pushing me over and over again and has invested in this dream of mine.

You prayed with me and believed in me and didn't let me give up.

Thank God for my two sons, Journee and Paxton, who have changed me from the inside out and continue to make me want to fulfill all that God has set out for me to do on this earth.

I want to acknowledge Eddie James who took me in at 19 years old and allowed me to use my gifts when I was still very broken and unaware of my identity. You let me preach and sing and share the gospel from a place of grace and the way you loved me forever changed how I see God's love for me.

Thank you, Rodney Mullins, for hearing the Voice of the Lord who has called out this vision into my life and has been a huge supporter of me in every season.

INTRODUCTION

Everyone has a story. Now, more than ever, this generation has been given all the tools to show people what it is we want them to see rather than who we really are. Through filters, bios, and presets, our version of our story has changed to fit the mold of what people define as successful and likable.

So, we Mask.

We cover the things that have made us who we are today. We sweep our pain and hurt under the rug and instead of dealing with what is really in our hearts. We turn to platforms where we can show the scripts that keep people following our made-up storylines.

But what if we Unmasked? What if we showed people who we really were, without all the filters that cover what it is we don't want people to see? When I chose to Unmask, it changed everything about the way I lived my life.

Listen, friends, I had some ugly things that were definitely worth hiding, but when you live in shame, you aren't living the life God has called you to live.

Being vulnerable helps us to find our truth … and your truth is your Superpower. I pray that, as you follow along with my story, you will be empowered to find your Truth.

The goal of Unmask is to get to the bottom of the façade and to deal with the unedited truth. My deepest prayer is for everyone to truly understand their identity in Christ so that they can begin to walk in their God-given identities. Your mess is just pages away from becoming your message. Let's take a journey together through vulnerability and let's Unmask.

CHAPTER 1

THE GIRL BEHIND
THE MASK

"Who are you?"
If I were to ask you that question, how would you answer? What would you say? Any time someone asks us who we are, we usually start rattling off the things that we do. "I am a mom, a wife, a homemaker, a teacher, a banker" … or whatever it is that helps you to identify yourself.

I am guilty of this also. Many times, I find that my identity is wrapped in *what I do* rather than *who I am*.

My bio on my social media platforms describes me as a wife, mom, worshipper, and blogger. (It's a fancier way of saying diaper changer, laundry enthusiast, chaos coordinator, and late-night creative …

and even that sounds fancy in place of what my actual reality is.)

Who we are often describes what we do, but it doesn't define us – even though it may often feel that way.

It is also common that we associate who we are with what we have been through in our lives. We tend to define ourselves by our worst moments or by trauma that we have experienced in our past.

I often wish that my life looked just like it does on Instagram – as perfect as those little filtered squares that I put out for everyone to see. If I can be honest (which you're going to find that I will be throughout this entire book, so hold your reins), I have always cared *way too much* about how people see me, my life, my family, and my accomplishments.

I would be lying if I said that the likes and comments of friends and strangers didn't make me feel validated and affirmed.

I have learned that I can navigate my life just like social media; I can mask what's going on with the filters of a smile, confidence, and bravery. It's easy, isn't it? We can show just a tiny little corner of our lives that looks perfectly put together when the entire room is falling apart. I mean, haven't you done it too? Pushed your unfolded laundry to the side to capture the "perfect" moment?

We know how to show people what we want them to see about us by angling the camera just the right way to show our "picture perfect" lives/lies. I am guilty at times of showing people what I think will get more applause than what will make me look vulnerable, and human. It's in our nature to want affirmation and validation; however, when we begin to idolize these natural human traits, we begin to lose ourselves.

So, who are we behind the masks? Who are we behind filters and façade that we so desperately want others to believe about us? Who really is behind the mask that we want ourselves to believe that we are? What will it take for us to start dealing with all the junk behind the mask – our heart issues and insecurities? Will we face it, or will we put lipstick on, add a filter, insert an inspirational quote of some sort, and wait for validation while covering our pain and sadness in the closet where we think no one will see it?

Will we continue to portray that our marriage is perfect and that our children are perfect, or will we face the music – realizing that no matter what we put out for the world to see, God knows us, has known us, and loves the person behind the mask?

The bottom line is that *God can't heal what we try to hide.*

You may be able to fool the world, your friends, and maybe even your spouse for a short time but eventually, just like any closet with junk in it, it begins to spill out and will eventually expose itself.

So, what do we do about these hidden places, these pieces of ourselves that we try so hard to hide?

We let God help us unmask.

I want to bring you on this journey with me to unmask the lies of the enemy so that we can find out who we really are.

This journey for me was ugly and painful. Many people had to watch me walk through healing and know what it took for me to get to the other side. This process is not for the weak or the faint at heart, so let's get real. I hope that, as I am honest with you, you will find a way to get honest with yourself.

It's time to unmask.

My earliest memory of putting on a mask was in the second grade when I lied about my middle name. I stood in front of my class and decided my sister's middle name was way better than Rae. I thought Rae sounded like a boy's name, so Renee was my stolen identity for the day.

This wouldn't be the first time I stole my sister's identity (but more on that later).

My childhood – just like yours – holds many memories; some amazing, some not so great, but each part of my story has made who I am today.

I learned to hide who I was and how I felt at a very young age, often because I didn't want people to see my reality. A couple of days before my seventh birthday, I rode bikes with my sister down to a local convenience store where we would get these jumbo-sized popsicles. It was a normal summer ritual; we would walk in the store with just enough money for our popsicles, then jump back on our bikes and pedal home as fast as possible so we could eat them out on the front porch. Blueberry was my favorite flavor.

This early afternoon, as we made our way to the checkout line, I saw my older sister grabbing a newspaper from the stand. She was acting secretive as she flipped through the pages.

I looked over and saw, clear as day, my dad's name on the front page of the paper.

I didn't ask any questions, but rode home knowing that it was something I wasn't supposed to see. Hours later, my cousin explained to me what the local paper had written. And that was how I found out that my dad – a pastor and the superhero of my life – had cheated on my mom.

I spent the next 10 years of my life trying to hide the fact that my dad was gay from everyone around me. My own identity became wrapped up in what had happened to our family.

This unexpected storyline wasn't what any of us had expected.

Before that day, I felt like I had the perfect life. I mean, who doesn't have the perfect life at six years old? But seriously, we had it all: Disney vacations, a pool, any Barbie doll we could have ever wanted! I was a pastor's kid living her best life, singing, changing the slides for songs, and repenting weekly in fear of the rapture taking place.

But in a moment, everything I knew and loved was taken away. I had no idea that for the next twenty years I would battle associating *who I am* with *what happened to me.* I hated the way the church looked at us, the way people felt bad for us.

Feeling ashamed of my family dynamics and not sure why they had to be the way they were, I began to mask the pain. Trying to hide from everyone how I was really feeling.

In my attempts to mask my anger and pain the best that I could, I began to add layer after layer to cover what I felt. I tried to be the "IT" girl and prove that I had it all. I wanted to be the best and tried to look my best, constantly begging for the world's affirmation of me. I felt like if I was smart enough, pretty enough, or rich enough, it would mask what I was feeling inside. The tables quickly turned as I spiraled into low self-esteem.

At fourteen, I found myself in a toxic and abusive relationship. I was in the ninth grade dating a high school graduate who for the next two years groomed me into believing that love equaled sex and control. This relationship affected almost every subsequent relationship I had. I lost all respect for myself; I was drawn to people who treated me poorly and I was completely dysfunctional after two years of ongoing abuse.

I wish that were the end of my pain, but unfortunately, it was just the beginning. I spent the next five years of my life in and out of terrible relationships. I partied until I couldn't remember. I drank until I couldn't feel. I lost myself.

Who was I?

I was the girl who never dealt with her pain. No mask, no filter could cover the tragedy I had become. It never failed that, after a short matter of time, the mask would always fall off.

Pain, anger, and unforgiveness would surface.

As soon as people get close to me, they would see how broken I was. The girl behind the mask never forgave her father for what happened. The girl behind the mask was terrified of God's love because she felt too filthy to be loved. The girl behind the mask had no idea who she was in Christ, or that she could even be given a new identity. The girl behind the mask was desperate to be whole.

At the age of nineteen, I began a long journey with the Lord to unmask and heal from everything I have ever been through – the abuse, the rape, the toxic relationships, the addictions, the pain. He met me right where I was, and just like He did with the woman caught in adultery,

Jesus got down in my dirt and began to transform my life.

There were so many layers to remove and it took years to bring me to where I am today. Today I am whole, healed, and living in complete freedom. I believe that no matter where you have been, you can have that too. I want to show you that if you allow God to heal your life, you can have all that God has in store for you!

"Therefore, if anyone is in Christ, the new creation has come: The old has gone, the new is here" (2 Corinthians 5:17).

Aren't you grateful that the recipe of a new life is simply being "in Christ"? I know we like to overcomplicate things and create in our head a checklist of tasks – simple and complex – that we believe might make us worthy of this new life. But the scripture promises exactly what it states. If we can find our identity in Christ, He will give us all the tools we need to live out our new life with not even a stain from our past to be found. If we don't find our identity in Christ, we will end up having access to the wrong things.

Let me give you an example. When I was 16 years old, I again stole my sister's identity ... but this time it was to get into a club. I remember standing outside in a long line repeating to myself her address over and over in hopes of not getting caught. Surely, I did NOT look twenty years old but there I waited with my jeans that had rhinestones on the back pockets, a tank top that was decked out in silver sequins, stilettos, and a borrowed coach bag.

The only thing I had going for me at that moment was the fact that my sister and I both had bleach blonde hair at that time. My palms were sweating, and my throat grew as dry as the Sahara Desert. A few moments later… I was in. That's right, I passed as my older sister and I was in a club feeling so cool, and slightly terrified. About an hour into being there, the purse that I had borrowed from my best friend was stolen. This included my wallet, my sister's ID, and my car keys. Talk about a FAIL.

This is not how I saw the night going. The problem was that, because I was using someone else's identification, I was given access to things that were not for me. I wasn't ready to be at a club or drinking. Heck, how was I supposed to know if I left my purse at the bar while I used the restroom that someone was going to steal it?

When you take on the identity of anything other than who God has called you to be, you will find yourself inheriting things that were never meant for you. You were never supposed to have shame, but you do because you didn't know who you were. You weren't supposed to end up in that bad relationship, but it happened because you took on the identity of someone who you felt you had to be, in order to be loved.

If you don't know who you are, it will affect your life and the life of every single person who is attached to you. (No pressure there, right?) Let me tell you, friend, that God is not playing when He tells us He knows us … not the person we have tried to be or have masked … but the *real* us.

God knows the *real* you

"Before I formed you in the womb, I knew you; before you were born, I set you apart; I appointed you as a prophet to the nations" (Jeremiah 1:5).

The person behind the mask is who we must find so that God can give us back our identity. We cannot do anything in life if we don't know who we are or – more importantly - Whose we are.

Have you been hiding what God wants to heal?

Do you mask it by not talking about it or hoping that the pain will one day disappear?

You may not have been through all that I have, or maybe you have gone through even more. God can change you the same way He changed me; I truly believe that.

Let's continue along my journey as you read to see how, layer by layer, God helped me to unmask the things that were holding me back from being all that God had called me to be.

How He transformed my identity by removing one false layer at a time.

"Vulnerability is not weakness; it's our greatest measure of courage."

— Brene Brown

CHAPTER 2
UNMASK THE VICTIM

In the first chapter, I shared with you that at the age of 19 I began a journey in which the Lord began dealing with my heart. Leading up to that time (just a few weeks before, to be exact), I was in hair school, working at Applebee's in the evenings, and dating a guy out of loneliness.

On a normal weekend, you could find me in a club. After just a few cranberry and vodka, I would be dancing on the stage, thinking I was one of Beyoncé's backup dancers. As I write this, I can't help but feel completely embarrassed, but I told you I would stay honest, so there you go.

My whole life flipped upside down when a weekend visit to my mom's turned into a come-to-Jesus meeting where I made a bargain with the Lord. Here was my bargain: "God, I know that there's more to this life and that I should change the way that I'm living, but I can't break up with my boyfriend, so if you have him break up with me, I will leave everything and serve you for the rest of my life."

Long story short, I come home from my trip and my boyfriend breaks up with me because of my new piercing. It was a Marilyn Monroe and everyone in hair school was doing it. (Seriously, you can't make this stuff up.) As promised, I packed everything up in my tiny car and moved back to my mom's house. Everyone in my circle of friends thought I had surely lost my mind.

That same week, I attended a church service that changed my life. I sat there with tears rolling down my face as members of a ministry team, one by one, began to share how God had set them free. Free from drug addiction, free from pornography, free from abuse, free from their past. They worshipped and they were unashamed, and I wanted what they had. I closed my eyes and knew I could never go back to the life I once lived.

One week later, I made the decision to live out of a suitcase, join this traveling ministry, and travel the world with them. If they hadn't been before, by this point people were really thinking I was nuts. In a couple of months, my profile pictures went from bar pictures to pictures of me riding camels around the Egyptian pyramids while in Egypt on a ministry trip. God works in funny ways.

I have no idea how I got to do all this. Looking back, it's crazy that one week I was in the club and the next week I was on stage telling people about Jesus and sharing my story all over the world.

The first time I gave my testimony, we were in Virginia Beach at the church of my aunt by marriage, Bishop Anne Gimenez. I had never shared my story or even thought about what I would say if someone had ever asked me to.

With my eyes closed and my hands lifted high during worship, I felt a gentle nudge on my shoulder. As I quickly looked over, I realized it was a microphone and I was on the spot being asked to share my story.

So many thoughts went through my head. *What would my aunt think?* I felt ashamed of what I had been through and the things that I had done. I compared myself against the incredible pastor and evangelist who had impacted so many lives and knew I would look filthy in front of everyone. Filthy in front of people that I thought were important; I wanted to look together in front of them. I felt exposed but I knew it was time to finally unmask.

I don't remember exactly what I said, but I know that with many tears and an ugly cry, I got through sharing my story for the first time. As embarrassing as it was, I felt like a weight had completely lifted off me. I felt relieved, like I wasn't hiding anymore.

Because I had spoken the truth out loud, I felt that it could no longer eat up my insides and torment me at night.

"Once a secret is exposed, it loses its power."

I began to tell my story almost every night for weeks that turned into months. It never failed that after every service people would come up to me and say, "We are so sorry that you had to go through that." It may not have been an apology from all the people who had hurt me or abused me, but by telling my story, I began to feel justified. I had been a victim of my circumstances and somehow, I had gotten stuck there.

I wanted people to feel bad for me because I had felt bad for myself for so many years. My identity for the next two years of my life became "the girl who was raped." Now, looking back, I can't believe that I was clinging to that title. My identity was wrapped up in my past. I became known for the worst parts of my life and I was okay with it. I was okay with it because it made me feel vindicated.

I meet women all the time who identify themselves according to their past. The woman who is an ex-drug addict. The woman who has been divorced. The woman who used to be promiscuous. These women are moms, wives, career women, and Bible study teachers, yet no one sees past their past.

I remember when God told me to stop telling my testimony for a season in my life. After sharing my story for so many years, it was nothing for me to meet someone and immediately pour out my whole life story.

I felt like people needed to hear my story when really it was *me* that kept reminding myself of where I had been. The truth is, behind the mask, I liked being a victim and I liked that people felt sorry for me. Worse, I liked feeling sorry for myself.

Many of us, women especially, have faced some form of abuse or childhood trauma. The problem is when we use that challenging or horrific situation from the past as a crutch or an excuse as to why we can't grow as people.

- "God, I can't stay pure before marriage because I've been raped."
- "God, I can't trust a man because I have daddy issues."
- "God, I can't be open because I've been hurt before."

Excuses, excuses, excuses

If you find yourself making any of the statements, you might be stuck in a victim mentality. When you remain this way, people will eventually stop feeling bad for you and you will be the only one holding on.

I believe that so many people like to remain a victim because it releases their personal responsibility to take ownership over their own lives.

I am here to tell you today that *freedom requires responsibility.* If you continue to point the finger at someone over and over, you won't have to be responsible for your side of the story. I was good at blaming everyone for years as to why I was insecure or why I sought out love from men or why I was dysfunctional.

I was better at throwing all my shortcomings on the fact that I had this past that crippled me when, in reality, I was crippling myself. The truth is that even though I didn't have a pictureperfect family, I could still choose what my life would be like. I made poor choices. I went back to people who had hurt me. I drank and then got in the car and drove down the one-way street. No one forced my hand, and no one made me do it; even though I went through all these things, I also put myself through a lot.

It's vital that when we unmask, we allow God to fix how we view our identity. That we no longer live by looking at ourselves through the lens of what happened to us, but that we choose to see ourselves as who God intended us to be. When we remain victims, we take that baggage into every relationship we have in life. It affects how we see leaders, authority figures, friendships, and marriage. It can even affect our children. No child needs to see their mom insecurely complaining about her weight, her job, and their relationships as if everyone is out to get them.

When you give your mess back to God, He really can make you NEW.

When you need healing in your life to find freedom from being a victim, it is a lot like having a broken bone. I have never broken any of my bones but my husband tore his tendon on our honeymoon cruise. Yes, my first few months of marriage were spent with my new husband in a full-leg cast and crutches. Our early memories as a married couple involve me driving him around like a chauffeur.

Talk about romantic.

He only had to use his crutches for three months, thank God. Some of us choose to keep our mental and emotional crutches a lot longer. When we remain a victim, it would be like my husband carrying around his crutches every day after he no longer needed them so that everyone would know he had been hurt. If he had remained a victim of his injury, it would have continued to put the responsibility on me to drive him around.

Take Responsibility for Your Healing

You cannot walk around wounded for the rest of your life because of the things that you've been through. It sounds crazy, but people do this every day in their spiritual life; they hang on to injuries when Jesus already paid the price, wiped us clean, and has given us the power to overcome.

You can only go so far while holding onto the baggage of your past. I will never forget the last night I worked as a server for Applebee's before my huge life change. That night, the Lord decided to show me truly how to forgive. I had already made the decision that I was going to move back to my mom's house to get my life back on track.

Even though I had promised God that if my boyfriend broke up with me, I would go, I was still looking for signs that I was making the right choice. Around 11 PM, just an hour before closing, I saw three men walking through the door. When I took a second glimpse, my heart stopped. I was the only server still working that night and I had to serve the guy who had drugged me, taken advantage of me, and left me in my car at a gas station alone.

I had not seen him since that night. A few years had passed, but as soon as we locked eyes, I felt so shameful. I pulled it together enough to get through the dinner and made as little eye contact as possible. I couldn't wait for them to leave.

I hid behind my computer in hopes that they would leave cash and I wouldn't have to interact with them again, but seconds later he walked up to me as my head hung low. I'll never forget how shocked I was as he began to apologize for what he had done to me. He explained that he had given his life to the Lord and that he was sorry for anything he had ever done. He is now a man of God, married and working in the mission field.

This first step in my healing process was so necessary before moving forward into all the other layers that God needed to deal with. This lesson taught me that God doesn't just want to save the victim; He also died for the people who have hurt us along the way.

In order to continue your journey of unmasking, you cannot remain a victim. You must forgive those who have wronged you. And you must move on with life. You must forgive others and you must forgive yourself.

You can stay where you are, or you can see people in the way that God sees them and realize that everyone in this world deserves an opportunity to know Jesus – the only One who can make a victim into a victor.

I don't know about you, but anytime life gets hard (and let's be honest - that's about 90% of the time), when I don't feel my best or feel that I have had enough, I immediately have to pull myself out of this victim mentality. If I don't, I begin to feel sorry for myself and start blaming my upbringing, my parents, or anything that will eliminate my responsibility to take ownership of my life.

Maybe there are goals you can't seem to achieve because of things that have happened in your life, but how long will we blame our past and let it dictate our future? Don't mask your victim mentality by placing blame on your past. Your past is not why you can't move forward and succeed in life.

You may not have control of what happened to you, but you have complete control of what you make of it.

The enemy wins when we believe the lie that we are what happened to us. When we believe this, we begin to act on that lie by not going after our dreams or by believing we don't deserve the best. It has taken me almost five years to even write this book because the enemy would constantly remind me of where I have been and made me feel silly to even have this dream of being an author.

Who wants to read a book from a girl who is a Bible school dropout? Well, if you're reading this, I guess you did, and this book in itself is an example that you don't have to be what happened to you. God's plan is bigger than any attack from the enemy that will try to steal your voice.

> *"You're not a victim for sharing your story. You are a survivor setting the world on fire with your truth. And you never know who needs your light, your warmth, and raging courage." – Alex Elle*

CHAPTER 3
UNMASK INSECURITY

I will never forget the morning I woke up and was confronted with insecurity, face to face. While I was getting ready for school, staring deeply into the mirror, I noticed the largest thing I had ever seen. It was my nose.

I ran downstairs to my mom and my sister, crying and wondering why no one had ever told me about this whale of a nose on my face!

Of course, they tried to assure me that it was in my head and that I was crazy. The truth is, I may be a little crazy, but I don't have the smallest nose in the world for sure. I have no idea what happened that day that made me realize my nose was the biggest part of my face ... but from that day forward, I was self-conscious of my breathing machine. This insecurity remained for the majority of my life.

Insecurity is one of the oldest tactics of the enemy that we women continue to fall for over and over again. The enemy will use people to point out our flaws so that we focus on not being enough.

Insecurity is stemmed in comparison. How many hours a day do we spend scrolling on all forms of social media wishing that we had what somebody else has? We often think to ourselves, *If I could just have what they have, then surely, I would be happy.*

If I could just have her job, I would be successful. If my husband was just a little bit more like her husband, then my life would be easier. If I could make my child eat fruits and veggies like that other mom who cuts them up and puts them in those perfectly divided plates, then I would be a great mom. I am completely guilty for scrolling and comparing, which leads to insecurity, which leads to feeling like a victim … and it's the same cycle over and over again.

If I could be honest, I think I have been insecure my entire life. That's probably no shocker because many women are. I never felt like I looked the part. I never felt like I was the best at anything. I constantly compared my talents and abilities to everyone around me.

I felt like my siblings were more talented than me. I felt like my friends were prettier than me and had more money. As I grew into an adult, my biggest insecurity went from my nose to my imperfect teeth, and I'm not joking. I would spend hours crying about my smile, not wanting to open my mouth to smile for pictures.

Insecurity is Rooted in Identity

You are insecure when you don't know who you are in Christ.

Our insecurity is so much deeper than our vanity. There is a deep root inside of us that believes we are not enough the way that God created us. If we don't unmask insecurity and deal with the root of the issue, those small insecurities that we have about our looks will turn into something much greater.

Because I didn't know who I was and I lost my identity due to insecurity, I went from the young girl embarrassed about her oversized nose to a young girl who would give herself away in order to feel loved and accepted. I ended up in a vicious cycle of being insecure about being rejected to being even more insecure.

When I was 14, I ended up in a relationship where I was taught that sex equaled love. That to be loved, I had to give myself away. I believed and bought into this because I didn't understand my identity in Christ. I masked my insecurity with relationships and false confidence trying to convince myself and everyone else that I really was happy.

Insecurity Will Cost You Something

I would be a rich girl if I could get back all the money I spent on trying to maintain relationships with people who didn't really love me. When you don't love or value yourself, you end up losing a lot more than your dignity. You will lose friends, money, time, and growth. Insecurity will take you on detours in your journey and prolong the destination that is your destiny. My insecurity and lack of identity put me in so many different relationships that wasted my time and effort before – and, yes, even after – I gave my heart to the Lord.

I even portrayed a façade that I was coldhearted and I let people know that they couldn't hurt me, but it was just a mask. Everyone learns how to mask insecurity in one way or another. As I grow older and the more I find myself healed from my past, I realize how ugly insecurity makes people. You can spot a person that deals with insecurity from miles away. It affects how they speak to people and how they carry themselves, and it always exposes itself under pressure.

My journey in healing from insecurity is still an ongoing process. When I first gave my heart back to the Lord, He began to change everything about me. I no longer dressed like the girl who was crying out for attention. I was happier, and I was able to be nice to other girls even if I thought they may have had more than me.

Even what I posted on social media began to change. It was less about drawing attention to me and more about drawing attention to HIM. As God began to transform my identity, I stopped doing things that would tear down my self-worth.

I wish I could say that it doesn't creep up even now, but the truth is that I have dealt with insecurity in every season of my life. With each new season, new insecurities surface, and I have to deal with new things. Sometimes, I also find myself dealing with old things all over again.

No matter where you are in your journey with the Lord, you will always find people to compare yourself to. I went from hating how I looked to hating how I led worship compared to other students in ministry school. Even now I struggle against comparing how I parent or how much money I have in relation to other parents and people.

The enemy will continually try to make you feel that you are lacking something. He will even go as far to make you feel like God has blessed other people more than you and that the reason you can't get the same blessings as other people is because of your past or even your current shortcomings. Now, as a mother and a wife, I have realized that insecurity and comparison will always continue to present itself, but *I have a choice if I want to give life to those thoughts.*

The truth is, someone will always be skinnier, more educated, and richer than I am.

Someone is always going to take a better vacation then I can afford. So now I have a choice: Will I sulk and cry? Will I crash diet or max out my credit cards with money I don't have? Or will I realize that my journey is simply MY journey?

Insecurity is dangerous because it causes us to focus on ourselves. All these feelings and thoughts of not being enough continue to put our focus on our shortcomings and what we lack instead of all that God is doing in our lives.

We spend so much of our time trying to prove to the world that we are these people we portray on social media to the point where we aren't even people anymore; we are just brands. What brand are you trying to put out to the world? That you are a perfect size 4, with no real problems, issues, or struggles? Who the heck is that going to reach or help? I can tell you, 100% of the people I know cannot relate to perfection. Inward focus, comparison, and insecurity are all signs that we need healing in our lives.

Underneath the mask of a passive-aggressive coworker or a sarcastic family member lies insecurity from that person's journey.

We must recognize that hurting people hurt people.

But if we allow God to heal those places in our hearts, we will not only see ourselves the way God sees us, but we will also see others the way that God sees them.

"Do not conform to the patterns of this world, but be transformed by the renewing of your mind. Then you will be able to test and approve what God's will is in his good, pleasing and perfect will" (Romans 12:2).

Part of seeing yourself through God's eyes is allowing God to change the way that we think. The patterns of this world tell us that we are not enough. How many commercials do we see a day telling us that we could be better, look better, and feel better? The patterns of this world tell us to pursue the American dream and we will be happy and successful.

The patterns of this world say to market yourself for followers, likes, and comments and you will then be influential. When we renew our minds, we can look through the lens of our heavenly Father. In His eyes, there is no comparison or contest. We can try and hide as long as we can, but I will tell you the insecurity will continue to surface in every season of life.

Insecurity Is a Form of Self-sabotage

I wish I had space in this chapter to list all the jobs and positions that I lost because of my insecurities.

Because of the times I felt intimidated about my lack of knowledge or education, or because I felt deep insecurity and it made me untrustworthy. Insecurity will only block blessings of jobs, friendships, and community.

You will end up on the sidelines watching others run the race when you focus on the kind of shoes that you have to run in. The way to unmask and overcome insecurity is by focusing on your own race. And if you keep your focus on Jesus, you will not have time to be inward-focused and insecure.

Life is so much better when you don't need everyone's approval and validation to feel successful. Life is so much fuller when you're living it instead of trying to post what you want others to perceive that your life really is. I don't know about you, but I want to love who I am more than I love what social media portrays me to be.

I don't want to SEEM confident; I want to BE confident.

I don't want to SEEM like a good mom; I want to BE a good mom.

I don't want to SEEM like I am spending time with God; I want to ACTUALLY BE SPENDING time with God.

Don't let your identity get tied up in what you aren't. Instead, ask God who He says you ARE. Unmask, face your insecurities, and let God deal with the root of the issue so that you can be who He's called you to be.

"Comparison is the thief of joy." – Theodore Roosevelt

CHAPTER 4
UNMASK REJECTION

To unmask and find your identity, you must be able to deal with rejection. I have experienced rejection on many different accounts in my life. One year sticks out to me the most; I felt like the entire theme of my year was BIG FAT REJECT. (Maybe that's a little harsh, but it sure felt true at the time.) That year was extremely hard for me and it almost took me out of the race.

I was in a new city around new people, and I had no idea that I was about to embark on one of the most challenging tests of my journey. I was in my second semester of Bible school in Dallas, Texas, when I had finally met a good guy. Based on my previous relationships where I dated mostly abusive, cheating losers, I realized I needed to date someone who loved God and would love me in a Godly way.

I didn't realize that most of the girls went to Bible college to get their "MRS" degree, but it didn't take long to pick up on the trend.

I was in my early 20s and ready to experience what it would be like to date someone who lived for the Lord. There was a guy in my school who began to show an interest in me, and he was no one like I had ever dated. He took me out almost every day, held every door we walked through, and would even buy me things that I liked when we were out at the mall. I had never been in a relationship like this before. I mean, technically, we weren't "in a relationship" but I assumed it was going in that direction since we hung out almost every day for months.

While hanging out with him, part of me felt like I didn't deserve the way he treated me.

His respect and kindness were like this foreign concept that I tried to understand and grasp.

But not long after I was feeling really good about the direction things were going, one day everything shifted. I walked into the cafeteria and I saw him standing in our spot talking to a new girl. My heart dropped because I already knew what to expect.

Within days I saw him doing everything with the new girl that he had previously done for me. And he gave me no explanation. The first guy I liked in Bible School dropped me like I was a hot potato

– or worse – and left me to internally pick myself apart and try to figure out what was so wrong with me. She was in and I was out.

The rejection I felt from that relationship sent me on a downward spiral. Normal people who know who they are and understand their identity in Christ may have been able to quickly dust themselves off, get back up, and try again ... but I completely flopped. That rejection brought out all the insecurities that I thought I had already dealt with.

Shortly after this took place, I began skipping class. I started gravitating toward guys who were similar to the ones I had hung out with before. My old habits hadn't died completely, and I saw myself slowly going right back to where I started.

Rejection Keeps You from Progress

I wish that I could go back and tell that rejected 21-year-old that I was going to meet the most amazing guy on the planet in three short years in my tiny hometown, that he was going to make me the happiest woman alive, and that he would be the best father and best husband I could have ever asked for. But at that moment, I couldn't see the future. All I could see was that I was not enough.

But the stream of rejection wasn't over. In that same year, at that same Bible school, I was hired to work at a well-respected ministry upon my arrival in Dallas. After a couple of days of training and a failed personality test, I received word that I was unqualified for my position. I mean, who could even fail a personality exam? Apparently, it's a thing. And apparently, my personality was not fit for this job. Not only was my personality not fit for the job, but my skill set was also not good enough. I was so embarrassed when I quickly went from a job of high esteem and purpose to unemployed.

I didn't get to have a cool title anymore and I wasn't going to see any benefits from working for the dean of the school. Everything that I envisioned for that year in Dallas completely crumbled before my eyes. I finally decided to apply for a job at a tanning salon because, surely, I was good enough to at least work there (plus, who doesn't want free tans)? I might not have known how to type super-fast or write perfect, grammatically correct emails, but I couldn't fail in turning on a tanning bed and selling some bronzing lotion.

The rejection from losing my job from that ministry was so painful it killed all my pride and confidence. I felt so rejected by people that I thought were important at the time. I had no idea that, because of the rejection from a ministry job, the redirection would lead me to meet my incredible manager, Autumn, there at that tanning salon, whom I had the honor of leading to the Lord in our little corner break room.

Rejection Is Often Redirection

We never truly understand why the rejection is happening until we get to the other side and can see God's plan within the pain. Not only did I get rejected from the cool ministry job, and the cool Christian guy, but I couldn't even make the praise team! *I went from traveling the world singing backup for Eddie James and now I can't make the praise team?* I kept asking myself the question, *Why wasn't I good enough?*

I mean that's the reason things don't work out for us, right? It's because we aren't good enough. Okay, I know that's not true, but it would almost be easier if that were the answer. Not being good enough would bring clear understanding as to why some things don't work out in life. But as seasons began to change in my life and as I grew in my true identity – as I learned to unmask, I realized something very important …

Rejection is Protection

It wasn't always that I wasn't good enough. Sometimes I was just trying to wear a shoe that God didn't want in my closet. The enemy uses rejection in our lives to make us feel like we are not enough. When we don't get the job we want, or we don't land the relationships we feel like we deserve, our immediate thoughts are that we are not enough. Anytime I have been rejected by anything in my life, I have always seen that down the road God brought a far better gift than the very thing that I felt rejected by.

At the moment, you feel like you lost something, and rejection will always make us feel like we are unworthy. But when you feel unworthy, always remember that *Jesus died on the cross to make you worthy.* Your actions, your past, and even your current title do not define who you are. Only God can define who you are, and He is the best Father and the Author of your story. Only He knows what is best for you.

> *"Before I formed you in the womb I knew you and approved of you as my chosen instrument, and before you were born I consecrated you to myself as my own, I have appointed you as a prophet to the nations" (Jeremiah 1:5).*

I don't know about you, but when I read that scripture, I am reminded that every time I choose something for my life without consulting the Lord, it fails. But every time I let God (who designed me before I was even in my mother's womb) conduct my life, it always works out. Sometimes we fear giving this power over to God, as if by our own decisions we can keep ourselves safer than God can keep us. But it's important to remember that God is never going to withhold a good gift from you.

Even though it may seem like it's something that you want or something you deserve, rejection is always protection. God's plan is way bigger and way greater than any plan we could ever come up with ourselves. So next time you don't get that position you wanted, or you don't get recognized, or you're not picked to be on that team, remember that it's for your good.

You may not see the good right away but if you trust God and trust His plan, He will prove to you that you are more than enough. God's plan for my life was always my amazing husband even though I experienced rejection from so many other men in my life. God's plan was for me to meet Autumn and to lead her to the Lord even though I felt like a complete failure for having to work in a tanning salon during ministry school.

When you unmask rejection and accept your identity in Christ, you will no longer feel rejected from the wrong things. Let God open the doors that are for you and close the doors that aren't part of your story. I promise you that He knows best.

"If you then, evil as you are, know how to give good gifts to your children, how much more will your Father who is in heaven (perfect as he is) give good and advantageous things to those who keep on asking him" (Matthew 7:11).

"Sky and earth will pass away but my words will not pass away" (Matthew 24:35).

"Be strong and courageous and firm; fear not nor be in terror before them, for it is the Lord your God who goes with you; He will not fail you or forsake you" (Deuteronomy 31:6).

God is FOR YOU, not AGAINST YOU.

Don't let a closed door make you feel rejected and not good enough. Don't take to heart a closed door from someone who doesn't know your beginning to the end. Don't worry about people who aren't concerned with your protection or anyone who is not connected to your journey.

In order to take your next step, you must deal with the rejection that has held you back!

"Rejection is protection for something that is greater to come."

CHAPTER 5
UNMASK SHAME

I want to start this chapter off by stating that this is by far the hardest chapter that I've had to work on in my book. Five years ago, when I felt led to share this part of my story, it was not popular to openly share about any kind of sexual abuse. I am so grateful for the #METOO movement and the platform that it has given many women to be able to share their stories of sexual assault. I have been blessed having the opportunity to see so many women become free by sharing their stories.

On that same note, I am very aware that there are also situations where women have used this movement to convict men who are not guilty of instances that were consensual. That's why I am very careful when writing this part of my story to let you know I am not just another girl who experienced sexual assault; this part of my journey is significant to the complete work that God did in my life.

My heart is never to shine a light on anything unless I feel like it could help someone in their own walk with the Lord. I take complete ownership in my part of the situations that happened to me. And it's important for me to state this upfront because I don't want my words to be tainted by the filter of me being a victim, or for anyone to assume I don't realize my part or role in the things that have happened to me in my life.

Now that that's out of the way, let me take you all the way back to my sophomore year in high school. I had just moved to a brand-new city. My mom and stepdad were pastors of the church in town and I had just come out of a terribly abusive relationship. Through the brokenness of what I had just been through, I found myself making more bad choices in one year than I had made in my entire life.

It feels like a complete blur, looking back. I can't clearly remember everything that happened. I felt so emotionally numb that I did not care about being loved, valued, or respected by anyone.

My self-esteem was at an all-time low and my relationship with the Lord had pretty much dissipated into nonexistence. I was so hurt and frustrated and I did not understand who I was. I didn't know how to tell men, "No." I don't even know how to explain how I felt as a young girl, except that I felt a deep obligation for the enjoyment of others and their happiness – even if it meant sharing my own body.

I found myself completely degrading myself over and over and wanting to get out but not fully understanding how to break the cycle. On two different occasions in the space of about a year and a half, I was assaulted against my consent. For many years I battled with the thought that it was my own fault. I mean, let's be honest, it's easy to sit back and hear all the stories about sexual assault and immediately think, *Well, why did you get yourself in a situation like that?*

The truth is, I put myself in situations and around people where this was bound to happen. In that one year, I had surrounded myself with an unhealthy environment and was engaged in a lot of recreational drugs. It would be a normal weekend to not remember what happened. With these two incidents, I remembered what happened. I remembered that there was nothing I could have done at the moment to get myself out of it.

At the time, I had even convinced myself that I deserved it. But there is something so different about giving something away versus having something stolen from you without consent. And anyone who has ever experienced this will completely understand that statement. I kept my mouth shut for years about this happening mostly out of fear that people wouldn't believe me. I never wanted to look like the girl crying out for attention over situations that I had put myself in.

Even though it's not easy to talk about and it's killing my pride to put these words on paper, it's a real part of my story and God had to teach me how to unmask the shame. The shame that followed the sexual abuse that I experienced was so much worse than the actual moment of abuse. That shame continued to pop up in my life and take precious moments from me.

That shame and those images would intrude in my mind when I was in worship. That shame would follow me around after I met my husband and make me feel like I wasn't worthy of someone like him.

Shame Makes Us Feel Unworthy

I can't tell you how many times that shame has interfered in my life and kept me from being all that God has called me to be. The cycle of shame is set up so that it continues to condemn you for things that God has already forgiven you from. Shame will continue to take us out of the race every time we believe the lies of the enemy.

In the early weeks of dating my husband, it was very clear to me that his past was in no comparison to mine. I knew God had called me into ministry and that I would do it with my spouse one day, but the thought of telling him about my past made me so fearful. I knew Ryon was going to be my husband pretty early in our relationship, so I did all that I knew to do: I tried to self-sabotage the situation so I wouldn't get hurt.

I thought, surely, if I told him my past – the things I did – the good, the bad, and the ugliest (that won't even make it into this book), he would show himself to be like other men in my past. He would realize I'm too much to take on and walk away. And who could blame him?

So, the day I decided to tell him my past, when I expected him to leave or start treating me differently, he did something completely different. He stayed. Not only did he stay but he respected me and valued me, to the point where I thought he was even friend-zoning me. It's funny now, looking back. I remember crying to my pastor's wife saying, "He will barely kiss me!"

This love he had for me was different than any other love I had experienced. God's love healed me, and He healed me by bringing my husband into my life. I know this doesn't fit the whole, "You must be healed before you married," sermon that is often preached. I wish that could have been my story that he would have met me when I was whole. But, that's not my truth.

My shame caused me to hide behind masks that wouldn't let people see where I had been. We mask our shame with our careers, our accomplishments, and the image we portray in order to be accepted and loved!

Shame Makes You Hide What God Wants to Heal
Let's talk about the very first account of shame in the Bible. What did Adam and Eve do as soon as they ate from the tree? They realized they were naked, and they were ashamed. They ran to hide because they knew they were exposed … but you can't hide from God. Ever since, we have tried to mask it. While they covered themselves up with twigs, we cover ourselves up with masks. We hide the pain, and we try to hide from God.

He said, "I heard the sound of You in the garden, and I was afraid because I was naked; so I hid myself" (Genesis 3:10).

The enemy uses shame to steal your fruit!

Shame is so much less about us and so much more about making sure that we don't reproduce! The very reason it has taken me five years to write the book God told me to write is because the enemy comes to say …

- *Who would read a book from a Bible school dropout?*
- *You're just a stay-at-home mom now. No one is going to read a book from someone who takes care of babies all day.*
- *There is still some residue from your past. People can tell you are still broken and the people who respect you now may not if you are TOO honest!*

These are real weapons of shame that I dealt with. As time went on and I found a new reason to be unworthy of writing this book, I realized all the enemy was doing for the past five years was distracting me from producing. I believed the lies, felt the shame, and stopped doing what God called me to do.

All the enemy must do to win is make us believe his lies enough to where we STOP. If you deal with shame from anything in your life – pornography, divorce, the debt that you have up to your ears, ongoing shame from not being obedient to what God has asked of you – I am here to tell you that SHAME is not a real thing. God didn't create it!

That means those feelings and thoughts are all pure lies from the enemy, who is scared that you might one day become the person God intended you to be.

You must pull yourself out of the cycle of shame. Otherwise, just like I had to, you will wake up five years later and realize your life is on hold because you fell for the enemy's plot.

God is so much bigger than our shame. You can mask it by trying to look successful or portray that you are doing whatever it is God wants, but at the end of the day God sees it all and He died for it. Think of that … God died for your shame!

If you are dealing with shame in your life, I want to challenge you to read and claim these scriptures over your life until it's gone!

> *"For God did not send his Son into the world to condemn the world, but in order that the world might be saved through him" (John 3:17).*

> *"But the Lord God helps me; therefore I have not been disgraced; therefore I have set my face like a flint, and I know that I shall not be put to shame" (Isaiah 50:7).*

> *"Those who look to him are radiant, and their faces shall never be ashamed" (Psalm 34:5).*

I love how the last two verses promise that if you look at God, you won't be ashamed. That is the key to unmasking shame; it's not looking at yourself, your past, and all your mess. It is looking at God who died for your mess and has forgiven you!

He doesn't see you as the daughter who was raped, divorced, broken, or abused. He sees you as His beloved daughter whom He loves, believes in, and has a plan for.

"Shame is the most powerful, master emotion. It's the fear that we're not good enough." - Brene Brown

CHAPTER 6
UNMASK FEAR

The mask of fear is one of the most common things that we try to hide behind. It can manifest itself in many ways. I believe that fear can be the root of all the other masks that I've worn.

- When we become a victim, it's because we are fearful to take on the responsibility of our new identity.
- Our insecurity can be rooted in fear of what other people think of us or the fear of never measuring up.
- The root of rejection can look like a fear of failure or unworthiness.
- Our shame can be rooted in the fear that we will never be enough.

If we don't deal with this one thing, it could be the very thing that will keep us from finding identity in Christ and becoming everything that God has called us to be.

I don't know about you, but I've dealt with fear my entire life. It's not always easy to put your finger on where it stems from, but it can cripple us – even in the smallest form.

It's common to be afraid of being hurt or disappointed. We fear failing in our careers; we fear that we aren't the mom or the wife that God has called us to be. We have a fear of not being good enough for the things that we feel God has called us to. The fears of losing control will paralyze us from stepping out in faith.

I can reflect on many moments of my journey to unmask. Looking back, I realize how many decisions I made based on fear. The moment that sticks out to me the most was when I was about to graduate from Bible College in Dallas, Texas. I went to chapel one morning and realized that my time in Dallas was coming to an end.

I had no idea what was next for me in terms of where I would live or what job I would have. I began to pray that morning and ask God to show me what He wanted me to do. That same day, just a few hours later, I received a text from my friend,

Ana. She texted, "Hey girl, I was just thinking about you. I had a dream last night that you moved back to Ohio."

The Holy Spirit opened my eyes at that moment, and I realized that He was calling me to move back home. I did not respond positively to that idea. *God, I prayed, how could you ask me to move back home? How can I go home to the place where I was living in sin and everyone knows about my past?* It was so much easier for me to move away and live for God in a place where no one knew about my past. In a place where I didn't have to prove myself or explain myself or look over my shoulder. I could just be this new person that God was molding me to be.

Even though I knew that God was asking me to move back home and start a ministry for women called "Unmask," I ignored His voice. I stayed in Texas.

I know that God had wanted me to step out in faith and start a women's ministry in my hometown, but I feared going back to the place where everyone knew me, the real me, not "Bible School Lyndsy" or "Worship team Lyndsy."

They knew the old me, and I thought I knew what they would think of me: "The girl who was broken. The girl who was wild and crazy." I believe that they would say, "The girl who was in the club just a few years ago is now a proclaimed preacher? What a joke."

How in the world could I go back to where I was from and hope people would take me seriously? I let fear enter my life at that moment, and I had no idea that it would send me on a huge detour.

When we yield to fear, it will add detours that prolong us from reaching our destination.

When we yield to fear, it challenges us to deal with the person behind the mask.

When I chose fear over faith, I found myself in Texas, in a relationship that was not from God, plugged in at a church that God did not call me to, and nothing was working out for me.

Why? Because at that moment, I had chosen to live in disobedience rather than to face my fears.

Here I was working as a full-time nanny, determined to make a size-5 shoe fit my size-7 foot. Nothing would fit! Not my relationship, not the church, and I knew that I was not where God had called or asked me to be. It began to weigh on me as the months went by.

When we live in fear, we will never feel fulfilled in what we're doing because we are living in the confinements of our own control.

Fear Will Keep You from Achieving Your God-given Destiny

After several months of living in fear in Texas, my heart couldn't take it anymore. I knew I wasn't doing what God had asked of me and I was paying for it in so many ways. I was just like the Israelites who knew the way to the Promised Land. Instead of trusting God, I whined, complained, and took the longer route.

Thank God It didn't take me 40 years to finally get where God asked me to go. But how many of us prolong the promises of God because of fear? On the other side of my fear, I had no idea that I would start a women's ministry with eight girls in my friend's living room – a ministry that would expand to six different cities around the world where women would meet and learn the material that God gave me about unmasking and finding their identity in Christ.

I had no idea that I would start an Unmask women's conference where women would come and have life-changing experiences after hearing my story. I had no idea that on the other side of fear, God had a wonderful man – who loved God more than me – waiting in my hometown to ask me to be his wife and give me the family I always wanted.

What if I had stayed? What if I missed it all? What if fear kept me from everything God had for me? The opinion of people almost kept me from all of God's promises over my life. And let me be honest, *no one knew I was living in fear.* I had painted the most beautiful picture on social media that my life in Texas was perfect and that I was thriving, when that was simply not the case.

I had masked my fear with trying to prove to the world that I had this awesome life I was portraying – with an awesome boyfriend, church, job, and blog ministry. No one knew how depressed I was because of my disobedience. No one knew that I was so unhappy in my relationship, or that I was the loneliest that I had ever felt. I masked that fear with a sense of pride and accomplishment that I was really making it on my own and had it all figured out.

Fear Will Make You Compromise

Have you ever thought about what *your* biggest fear is? What is the one thing that keeps you from becoming the person that God has called you to be? We must dig deep to realize what our fear is rooted in so that we can make sure that we are dealing with the issue and not the symptoms. The symptoms of fear are many and they might include …

- *Taking a job that we are overqualified for.*
- *Staying in a relationship when we know that God has a better plan for us.*
- *Not wanting to switch churches because we're comfortable with the things that we've always known.*

One of my symptoms prolonging the writing of this book for as long as possible. The root of my fear was that I still struggled with how people perceived me. Even now, this is not an easy fear to let go of.

If we don't know the core reasons of why we struggle, then we will never figure out how to care for the symptoms. The only way we can deal with the root of the issue is to ask God to renew our minds.

> *"Do not conform to the pattern of this world, but be transformed by the renewing of your mind. Then you will be able to test and approve what God's will is-- his good, pleasing and perfect will" (Romans 12:2).*

The concept of a perfect love can be very hard for some of us to grasp. I only ever knew a love that said action equals acceptance. My experience with love said, "If you get too boring, I will leave you and find something better." People who told me that they loved me had only cheated on me, abused me, and rejected me. This made understanding God's love for me very difficult.

What is it in your past that keeps you from receiving the fullness of God's love?

I wanted to be fearless and I wanted to live without restrictions, but my fear of being disappointed by God and being disappointed by myself kept me from trusting Him completely and stepping out in faith.

Fear Will Make a Way for Plan B
I have learned that there is God's plan for my life, but there is also a Plan B. We will typically make

Plan B on our own if we're in disagreement with God's plan.

Living in fear means that there isn't full trust and surrender to God. It means that we trust Him but we also have boundaries on that trust; we act as if *He* needs *our* help. We can pray to

God and ask Him to do something in our lives but if He doesn't answer us the way that we want Him to, we get fearful and try to manipulate things while putting God's stamp of approval on our own plans.

Fear wants us to settle and believe that we don't deserve more in life. If fear has kept you from your full potential for years, you can break the cycle now. You may mask fear with all the fleeting things this world has to offer, but if you are willing to unmask and find out where God wants you to be, you will begin to discover who He says you are.

"The only thing we have to fear is fear itself." – Franklin D. Roosevelt

CHAPTER 7

UNMASK AND OWN IT

On your journey to unmask and find your identity, the next part of your process will be learning to "Own it." That's right, first God will take you layer by layer and deal with all the issues of your heart that you're currently going through. After you deal with all the fear, insecurity, rejection, and pain, He will help you to uncover those wounds so that you can be healed from the things you mask that will only hold you back.

When it's time to own it, that means you are starting to understand that your story is part of who you are and what He's called you to. I'm not saying that what you went through had to happen for you to be where you are today, but I am saying *because it did happen,* now it's time to use your story for His glory.

Your Story for His Glory

You must own that your story is a part of who God has called you to be. The pain that you went through? The tough season that nobody knows about? All those things have worked to create the person you are today. You are strong because you made it through and now you're on the other side.

You are powerful because you decided to let God deal with all those issues in your heart that were keeping you back from becoming the person He's called you to be. Your story is not just for you; it's for the people who are around you and the lives that God has called you to impact.

When we reach the other side of our mountain and we allow God to set us free from the things of our past, it is then our responsibility to walk out our freedom and find our identity in Christ while bringing others on the journey with us. You have no idea whose life you will impact if you unmask and get real with one another.

In a world where everyone desires to look perfectly put together, you will never truly understand the impact that comes with being open and honest about where God has brought you from. As I have grown in my relationship with the Lord and as life has taken me into new levels – both personally and in ministry – I have found that it has grown harder and harder to share about who I used to be.

Sometimes when I share my journey, it seems so long ago; I feel like I'm telling someone else's story. It feels so amazing to be so entirely healed from all the junk that I've been through in my life to the point where at times I can't even remember the things I felt and how bad it truly was.

I have even found myself in different seasons not wanting to share my story for fear that people will see me as someone who is still broken and messed up. Yes, I am aware that this is pride and it's not from God, but when you have worked so hard to achieve the life you thought could never be possible based on what you've been through, it's not easy to bring up the pain that got you there.

It's important for me to remember that, as I continue to become the person that God has called me to be, my story and my testimony are not just for me. It's selfish of me to keep my testimony for myself.

The same holds true for you. People need to hear your story so they can have hope for where they are. I want to continue to own where I came from and help others own where they have been.

If You Own your Past, It CAN'T OWN You
What you have been through is not your identity. If we let our testimony define who we are, we will never bring people on our journey to show them the freedom that they can have when they give

everything to Jesus. Owning our story means being real about what it took to get where we are today ... just like I'm doing throughout this book.

If I wrote a book on how many times I failed trying to overcome the different things that the Lord was trying to pull me out of, that book would be at least a thousand pages. I haven't always got it right on the first try. I admit that there are many times I have taken the mask off only to put it right back on in fear of judgment. No one has become the person that God has called them to be without stumbling through the entire process.

Part of owning our story is owning our struggles.

Sometimes we even mask becoming who God has called us to be by hiding behind life events that we feel will make us feel complete or ready to be the person He wants us to be. I remember thinking ...

- *If I could just finish ministry school, then I will be the person God has called me to be.*
- *If I could just find a husband to love me and support me and be in this race with me, I would not struggle with insecurity and fear anymore. I would then be who God has called me to be.*
- *Once I'm a mom, then I will feel whole and be the person that God has called me to be.*

- *When I've begun a full-time ministry, then I'll be complete.*

When you unmask and you own your struggles, you will realize something both sobering and freeing: just because you have attained what society defines as success, it doesn't mean you won't struggle. There are struggles that you will have to face daily. You know those issues that you unmask and let God deal with? Sometimes they do come back.

After all, we are REAL people with REAL issues, and we can't hide the issues forever. For my entire life, I felt if I had the things that I knew God had promised me, I would no longer feel the side effects of not having my identity fully rooted in who God says I am. I assumed that once I became a wife and a mother and ministry leader, I would no longer deal with insecurity, comparison, rejection, and fear. Boy, was I wrong.

When I realized that I was going to continue to struggle in those areas, it finally made sense that it was less about the struggle itself and more about how I responded to the struggle.

And let's be honest, people, the struggle is real.

No one wants to live their life constantly dealing with things from their past that continue to hold us back from being the person that God has called us to be. No one wants to talk about the fact that they are still insecure in their marriage, or how we still at times continue to feel like we're not enough for the call that God has placed on our lives.

No one wants to own that, though we feel called to do something great, we can barely keep our emotions in check to fulfill our normal duties in life. The only way to fully overcome the struggle is to own where we are. Staying in denial about the fact that you might still struggle with things from your past will only continue to mask what's going on in your heart.

You can mask your insecurities with all the perfect moments that you captured on your iPhone. But as you put out your best moments on everyone's timeline, you must remember that God sees those issues in your heart. If you don't own your struggles and your story, you won't be able to continue in your healing process.

"And we know that in all things God works for the good of those who love him, who have been called according to his purpose" (Romans 8:28).

Perhaps you feel that your story and your struggles have worked against you in more ways than you can count. Maybe you feel that all those experiences will forever keep you from becoming the person God truly wants you to be. But read that verse again. Really internalize it. This scripture promises us that *everything* that seems to be working against us actually works *for* us when God's hand is in it. It even takes it a step further to say that all we have to do is love Him and He will take our mess and turn it into a message. How easy is that?

- Love the person that brought us out of the very pit that tried to ruin our lives.
- Love the person who loved us even in our ugliest moments.
- Love the person who loved us during our insecurity, rejection, fear, and shame.

The only requirement that it takes for things in life to simply work out is that we love God. Loving God means letting Him take us through the process. Loving God means yielding when He wants to deal with that junk that's in our hearts. Loving God means sharing about all the amazing things that He has done in our lives and using our testimony to help others in their journey. Loving God means leaning on Him even though we may continue to have struggles on our journey.

What if we lived our lives knowing that no matter what we're going through and no matter what happens, He is going to work it out? How much time would that save us from trying to figure out what's next or what He has in store for us?

It would save us all that time we spend trying to find the person we are supposed to be with or trying to do what God has called us to do. What if we learn to just rest in the fact that – because of our love for Him and His love for us – He is going to work everything out? I don't know about you, but this understanding has changed everything for me.

It reminds me that no matter how hard the enemy has tried to use my past against me, God is going to continue to take the mess and use it as a message to reach other people about His unfailing love and grace.

So, unmask by owning where you are.

Own your story and your struggles so that they can't own you.

That is the way to find your identity and become who you are called to be. That's what unmasking is all about. Staying real and raw about where you are and where you have been. When we keep our struggles inside, when we keep our story private, we mask what we've been through by not showing anybody the pain that we've encountered. We keep it all in and continue to fight the battle on our own.

But when you unmask and expose where you've been and how you struggle, the enemy immediately loses his power. Whatever it is that you feel might have power over you, it's time to unmask own where you are and let God continue to work everything out for your future.

> *"Confess your sins to each other and pray for each other so that you may be healed. The earnest prayer of a righteous person has great power and produces wonderful results"* (*James 5:16*).

"If you Own your Past, it CAN'T OWN you."

CHAPTER 8

UNMASK AND HEAL

I am no stranger when it comes to the healing process – both physically and emotionally. And as you have read some of my story, you will see that it's an ongoing process on my journey to becoming whole.

Healing can be tricky in the sense that there will be times when you feel healed … only to realize that wound is still very much there. Sometimes we mask the wound with layers that we use to avoid our true feelings. I am so blessed to be a mom to my two beautiful boys. My first son was born a week early through an emergency C-section. My second son was also born through a scheduled C-section just two years later.

After having my first son, when my surgery was over, I was lying on the bed and staring at the ceiling with no feeling whatsoever from the waist down. I was in total shock, having just gone through something I was totally unprepared for. My birthing plan went out the window and my body had a long road of recovery ahead.

I was thrilled to be a mom but immediately realized my limitations as my body recovered from my surgery. When my baby cried at night, I didn't have the strength to pull myself up to get him. I would have to push the button and call for a nurse just to help me feed my newborn baby who needed me. I was frustrated with my own limitations and even more frustrated that I felt I couldn't be there for my son in the way that I wanted to.

Healing Will Limit You

When you have a story or situation that God has delivered you from, for a season your healing will limit what you can do. This does not mean we aren't accepting that Jesus paid it all!

This means we must know what we can handle and when we need to ask for help. I have learned this the hard way one too many times in my own journey.

The problem is that we see the way other people perform in their marriages, or how they lead others so fearlessly, or how they're accomplishing all their goals, but we didn't get to see the journey that got them there. It's so important to stay in tune with the Holy Spirit and know what parts of your life still need to be healed so you don't move too quickly and get reinjured. This wounded part of you could be unforgiveness that still resides in your heart. It might be a situation that you haven't fully given to God.

If you want to unmask and heal, you have to know what you can handle in each season. If you just got out of a terrible relationship, give yourself some time to heal before jumping into another one. If you just experienced hurt from your leader or church, give yourself some time before serving in a high capacity again. It's okay if you need to take time for yourself so that the next time you walk through a door God opens, you are ready and capable of handling it.

Healing Requires Help

I admit, this part is hard for me. I hate asking for help! When I was healing and had to press that button to ask a nurse to help me so that I could be a mom to my baby, I was frustrated. No one wants to rely on other people to be who they were called to be. I was called to be a mom and God gave me that perfect gift, but there was a season when my healing limited my abilities.

Once I got home, I would get frustrated that I couldn't move the bassinet from one room to the other. I was sad that I couldn't pick anything up that was too heavy without my husband's help. For whatever reason, I've always related needing help with weakness. To an extent, that phrase is true. Because we are weak in certain areas of our lives, we will have to depend on other people to help us through that weakness so that we can be the person God has called us to be.

But God made us this way so that we must depend on Him and on each other.

This comes with putting our pride aside, realizing our limitations and where we are in our healing process and allowing other people to hold us up when we are weak. God has given us the community to help us through our healing.

Jesus never intended for us to do life alone. That's why, when you read through the New Testament, one of the first things Jesus does as He walks in His purpose is to start a small group of community.

Jesus brought 12 men along with Him on His journey. They saw the good and the bad. They saw Jesus when He was weak. They saw Jesus when He was casting out demons and performing miracles. They saw Jesus when He was afraid or tired, and that's what community is about.

Healing is about unmasking in front of people you can trust and sharing your life with them. It's not pretending that you're happy and have it all together; it's being honest and vulnerable about the fact that you're still healing and still figuring out life just one day at a time. Now, don't get me wrong. I can relate to being in a community where you feel like no one will ever truly understand where you've been.

The truth is, no one may ever understand the pain that you've endured and the things that you have had to overcome in your journey. But in order to walk in your God-given identity, you have to be willing to unmask and heal through the relationships that God will give you.

Those relationships may look different in different seasons of your life.

Maybe it's a mentor that you need who has been ahead of you in many things that relate to your life and who can help you to navigate the things that feel tough.

Maybe it's the church that you're committed to, yet you live in fear of being judged; you have yet to fully allow yourself to be who you are in front of them.

Maybe you need a counselor who can help you sort out things you have been through and why you're still dealing with them in your adult life.

Needing help is okay!

God's Word promises us that, through our weakness, God is made strong. If you are feeling weak because of the things that you had to walk through in your life or the pain that you're still navigating, believe that God wants you to depend on His strength. You will never know the relationships that you are robbing yourself of when you hide behind a mask of a smile or a fake "I'm fine," when you honestly feel like you aren't going to make it through another day.

Our Scars are Reminders

If the stretching of skin wasn't enough to remind me of the birth of my beautiful boys, the scar from my surgery that perfectly separates my lower abdomen like a hot dog bun is. I know I shouldn't complain about the scars that gave me the best miracles in the entire world, but let's be human for a moment. What about my aspirations to get a six-pack or wear a two-piece at the beach again? Just kidding, I would never aspire for something that would require me to give up ice cream and pizza. (I mean, come on!)

But seriously! I thought I was recovering just fine from my surgeries only to be changing a diaper and get kicked in the lower abdomen and literally want to yell all the bad words out loud! Or those times I just wanted to sit on the floor and put a puzzle together with my toddler and get a sensation starting from the top of my neck all the way down to my cushion that felt like an electric shock to my spine.

If you have had a C-section, you are probably nodding along because that pain is no joke. You can run a marathon and be fine, but pick a toy dinosaur up off the floor the wrong way and you will turn every shade of angry! When you have walked through healing, you will be brushed the wrong way that may trigger you to remember the pain you once had. I used to think this meant I wasn't healed … but that's not true. It means that, as you are on your journey, you will always have reminders that you are a walking miracle.

You endured the pain and the process, you allowed God to heal you, but you will always be reminded of the pain so you will be able to see the victory. You could be in the greatest place you have ever been in your walk with the Lord yet the enemy will still try to use your scars to make you remember. To make you feel ashamed.

Yes, our scars can be ugly. It's natural to want to hide them from the world, but your scars are your testimony. The enemy means to use these scars for evil – to try and make you think you are still broken; you are still messed up; you still have issues from your past.

God sees those same scars and says, "Wow, Daughter, look how far you have come!"

If you want to heal, you must see your scars the way God sees them. You must unmask and stop hiding your beautiful story that could only ever be your story.

When I see other moms at the beach with their one-piece on and their slightly stretched skin, I never think, "Man! She should hide that!" or, "That poor woman had to lose her body to have those beautiful babies who are looking at her like she is their world."

No, I smile and nod and know that, right underneath my one-piece, I also have a story. And the story that left some marks gave me my beautiful boys whose toes are filled with warm sand and their hearts are overwhelmed by the joy of the ocean waves and smell of saltwater. It's at that moment where I can close my eyes and think … *"It was WORTH it!"*

Every scar was worth it – every amount of pain I endured and the rejection I faced. The shame I felt and the unworthiness and the attacks against my future. The breaking and healing process and the journey to wholeness. The love I learned to receive, the scars that I wear, the story that's my own. The pain brought me to who I am today. Now, as I continue to unmask and own my story, I will be able to heal and wear my scars proudly, knowing the process was meant to make me and not break me.

I made it to the other side. I embraced my truth. I took the mask off, and I committed to wholeness. Wholeness looks like healing and healing looks like grace to walk another day in the journey God gave you.

Sister, you are not alone, and your scars don't define you. Your identity isn't in the past pain that you have endured. It's in who God says you are through it all.

"We must be willing to let go of the life we have planned, so as to have the life that is waiting for us." – E. M. Forster

CHAPTER 9
UNMASK AND BE FREE

I'll never forget the day I met true freedom. I had come a long way from sobbing through my testimony at Rock Church the first time I had shared it. Where I was in my healing process really determined which part of my story would move me or make me feel some type of emotion as I would travel and speak. This day was different for me. I didn't get angry when I talked about my childhood.

Nothing moved inside of me when I talked about the abuse. I didn't feel sad for myself or even embarrassed. I didn't have to hold back my tears or try to keep a straight face. It was almost as if I was sharing someone else's story. After it was all said and done, I couldn't understand what was happening.

Have I grown cold? I asked myself. *Or shared so many times that it now feels like a broken record? Is it no as impactful anymore because there were no tears or emotions?* Nope, that wasn't it. It was freedom.

Healing brought with it a freedom that started to change how I shared my journey. I was no longer sharing from pain but from strength. I was no longer stuck in cycles of shame but walking in power.

Freedom was the destination throughout my journey, not perfection or the appearance of success. Through every layer that I had to unmask, I felt myself getting stronger, I felt my faith getting bigger, and I saw my eyes being opened to the person that God had always intended for me to be. I was no longer the girl with the story of brokenness, shame, and regret.

I was free.

Not only was I free from my past and the things that I had to go through, but I felt free to be me. I felt free from what others might think about me after sharing my story. Free from the opinions of people and from picking myself apart wondering if I had shared too much. I felt free from trying to hide certain details of my story and using masks to guard myself.

There was even a time when I thought if I wore my mask well enough that I might be able to protect myself from being rejected. I thought that by wearing masks it would keep me from being hurt or judged. It turns out that most of the time I was hiding behind these masks, I was actually hiding from myself.

I wasn't sure that, if I was truly vulnerable and exposed, I would even like the person who was hiding. I didn't want to be disappointed or fail to measure up to the idea of who I really wanted to be in this world. Coming from a life of dysfunction, all I ever really wanted was a "normal" story. Quite frankly, I believe that there have been points in my journey where I cared about the *appearance* of this more than really wanting it.

The desire of my heart was a beautiful family and a white picket fence with all the Instagram-able moments (insert hanging pot plants and the perfect white lighting for my photos). Freedom came with truly accepting my story. Accepting where I had been and where God has brought me to today.

My freedom came when I stopped comparing my life to other people and learned to be grateful for the life that God has given me. My freedom came when I chose forgiveness every single day and embraced that, although my life may not be perfect, God has grace for me and my family to walk out His purpose for our lives.

Your Truth is Your Weapon

When I was growing up there was a movie about a rapper; it was one of my all-time favorite movies.

I would like to disclose that there is no way possible my mom knew I was watching it and I am sure that I watched it because of my older sister. Now that that's cleared up, I want to take you to the end of the movie where there is an ultimate throwdown between one rapper and another.

They are going back and forth at each other when the main character realizes his opponent is about to go for the dirt that he knows about him. Instead of continuing the trend of bashing his opponent, he decides that he is going to use all the things that he knew this guy would say about him so that he would have nothing to use against him. He goes on to say, "I know I am trailer trash ... [insert a lot of other not-so-nice things]."

Don't start judging me on this amazing rap battle reference, as it relates to our freedom in Jesus! The point is that the enemy can't use your junk against you when you unmask. He wants you to stay silently bound, dealing with things alone and in the dark. He wants you faking it until you make it.

He wants you to push all those things that you are feeling deep into the closet and keep them far, far away. He doesn't want you to speak up and use your story to help others. Just like the rap battle, you can only win by taking the very lies that the enemy uses to defeat you and own them and walk in your freedom.

Yes, you were broken … but that's not who you ARE.
Yes, they left you … but you are not alone.
Yes, you aren't in control of what happened when you were a child … but this doesn't define your future.
Yes, you don't come from a lot … but God is blessing you.
Yes, you have made some wrong choices … but you still deserve God's best.

Don't keep your story hidden in the dark, because you can only develop in the light.

You can win your battles through honesty and vulnerability. I know it's scary to be vulnerable and to feel exposed, but your truth is your weapon. The best place you will find to fight your battles in life is in prayer and in worship.

"Where the spirit of the Lord is, there is FREEDOM"
(2 Corinthians 3:17).

If you want to be free and stay free, stay close to Jesus. If you want to move forward in your journey to find wholeness, get close to Jesus. When you unmask from everything in your life that was sent out to break you, God will be sure to make sure that it makes you!

Nothing about your journey is in vain when you unmask and use your testimony to reach others with the message of Jesus Christ. Friends, there is true freedom when we decide to let God see what is hiding behind our mask. Not temporary freedom where we go back to old habits or mindsets, but when we allow ourselves to be truly exposed, we can find truth that helps us to walk out our freedom every day.

"I could not imagine that the future I was walking toward could compare in any way to the past that I was leaving behind." — Nelson Mandela

CHAPTER 10

UNMASK AND BE WHOLE

Have you ever attempted to put something back together that has been completely shattered? I myself have broken a window, a lamp, and a couple of dishes in my lifetime (and by lifetime, I mean last week.) Well, maybe not all last week but I have had my fair share of accidents. I think it's fair to say that when you shatter something, it's not the easiest to put it back together.

Most things that are in tiny, itty-bitty pieces after the damage has been done will end up needing a full replacement. One of the things I have shattered more than once has been my iPhone screen. Thank God you can still usually use your phone with a broken screen. You would think after a couple of times

I would invest in a screen protector, but I like to live life on the edge!

On our journey to wholeness, we often look at our lives or situations as unrepairable. We see all the little tiny pieces lying there and can't even imagine how we could be put back together. We realize that even if we attempt to glue it, there is a big chance someone will still get cut. It's true that when you are broken, you end up hurting others along the way.

We do this mostly with our words and also through our lack of trust in people. Have you ever heard the statement that "Hurting people hurt people"? Well, it's true.

God never intended for us to be so broken; He wanted us to live a life of wholeness with Him where we never even knew about evil. He knew that if we lived life within the boundaries that He set, we would live our best lives. His intention for us always has been wholeness and closeness to Him.

Unfortunately, because of the fall of man, our wholeness is now a journey back to Jesus where we need to choose to be whole every day. Transformation of our mind, body, and soul is not a one-stop shop, contrary to popular belief. Wouldn't it be easier if the day we said YES to Jesus, we never had to battle our issues or pain again?

Most of the time the reason people can never get to the place of wholeness, where they are walking in their God-given identity, is because they decide that the journey is far too long and much too hard.

I don't know about you, but I am so glad that Jesus didn't give up on me when the journey started to get too long. I am so grateful that He never thought my process was too long or too hard. He stayed the course with me, let me make mistakes, and helped me renew my mind every step of the way.

Did my journey take way longer than it should/could have? For some things ... HECK, YES! Allowing God to give you a new identity, as amazing as that sounds, can be much harder than we think. Have you ever seen the reality TV show, "Hoarding"? (God bless those people; I mean, just watching the show makes me want to get up, clean my house, and throw a few things away.)

When they start interviewing people who live this hoarding lifestyle, it always comes down to the root issue that there was some trigger that made them start living this way. The reason usually comes out that the person experienced a death in their life that made them start keeping things. Because they cannot control what they lost, they keep everything they possibly can to hold on to a memory of how something once was.

If we aren't careful, we can become "identity hoarders" – keeping any proof possible of our old selves. When we meet Jesus, that person we once were has to die. But we hold on to that person because it's what made us comfortable. We hold onto it dearly because we lived in that mindset or circumstance for so long.

Are you fully embracing the new life God has given you? Are you unmasking in order to receive your new identity, or are you keeping souvenirs around of your past because it's what you KNOW?

The Lord has shown me over time that I need to look at wholeness as a puzzle piece and not as a shattered window.

Yes, you may feel shattered, but God knew what you would go through and already has this beautiful puzzle with thick, curved pieces ready to help you put it together. Wholeness starts with how you see God.

So, *how do you see God?* Do you see Him as an angry, frustrated God who gets mad every time you mess up? Do you see Him as someone who is passive about your problems and doesn't hear you when you're crying out? Do you see Him as a God that doesn't care when you're walking through hard times?

In order to walk in wholeness, you must know the character of God.

You know this when you build a history with Him. When He shows up in the scariest of moments and proves His faithfulness. When He blesses you and gives grace and mercy when you didn't deserve it.

To unmask and be whole, you have to make the choice to get to know God every single day. The way you view God will directly affect the way you view yourself. You are powerful and courageous, but if you look in the mirror and see weakness and brokenness, that means you need to look at God again.

How we look at our lives and what we believe about what we deserve says a lot about how "whole" we are. It's not to say that we don't acknowledge our weaknesses. You can see your broken pieces, but that doesn't mean you live from that place. Wholeness is living from the place of knowing who God is and knowing who you are because of His power.

I don't want to live another day thinking I don't deserve one of my dreams based on my past. I don't want to hide my dreams and desires behind a mask of mediocrity, thinking that I could never have or be the person God has truly called me to be.

Wholeness will determine what we do with how we see ourselves. Will we get the courage to start a blog, or to tell our story? Will we apply for the job that we feel underqualified to do? Will we find ourselves in unhealthy relationships based on a failure to understand our selfworth? Wholeness is not about striving for perfection. It is about finding rest in who and where we are in life.

Wholeness cannot be determined by our circumstances because damaging things do happen in life. We must be able to find comfort within the discomfort of how life feels.

Wholeness is not something that we can attain on our journey to unmask. Wholeness is a gift from God, and we have to show up and be brave enough to be vulnerable and accept this gift every single day. We can be whole because the One who made us is Holy. To live a life unmasked, we have to break the façade of Christianity and trust that our identity in Christ makes us whole and accepted in Christ.

I don't know about you, but I never want to live from a place of hiding again. Masking my pain is exhausting, but this life I have with Jesus now has transformed the exhaustion to energy and power. Fully unmasked, fully owning my place, and fully walking in my destiny is the point of the entire journey – to arrive in this place of full dependence on God.

> *"May God himself, the God who makes everything holy and whole, make you holy and whole, put you together – spirit, soul, and body – and keep you fit for the coming of our Master, Jesus Christ. The one who called you is completely dependable. If he said it, he'll do it!" (1 Thessalonians 5:23-24)*

"Our past may explain why we're suffering but we must not use it as an excuse to stay in bondage."

CHAPTER 11
LIFE BEYOND THE MASK

So how does the story end for the girl who lived behind the mask? I can tell you that, first and foremost, I am still far from perfection. It takes applying these steps over and over again to stay on track.

Life beyond the mask looks like total restoration between my father and me. I talk to him every single day and completely adore him. It's been a full restoration of my life and my family's lives.

When I sit back and watch what the enemy tried to take from us, I feel like I am at the NBA finals standing and cheering for the winning team when it comes to my loved ones. The enemy truly tried to use everything in his power to keep us all from walking in our God-given purpose, and here we all are, killing it!

Life beyond the mask has brought me to not only *understand* love but to be able to *receive* love and *give* love. Beyond my insecurities, beyond my past, and beyond my failures, I can still walk in my God-given identity. I live life from a place of worthiness. I approach God from a place of understanding that, because *He* is worthy, *I* am worthy. I don't have to live life on the sidelines or from the back row based on my past, but I now use the very things I once masked to put me in the game.

Life beyond the mask has made me realize that some people prefer the mask.

Vulnerability can make people uncomfortable, and as such, I may be judged when I share "hard" things. Guess what? You can only live *your* life and represent *your* story. People who can't handle your unfiltered life shouldn't get to show up for you only when things look pretty.

People who love the real you will stand with you no matter what. The dirty, ugly, raw things won't scare them. You won't be "too much" when it comes to finding your tribe. Life beyond the mask can sometimes be lonely if you haven't yet met other women who will share their journey with you.

Life beyond the mask for me requires continual evaluation (maybe to a fault). I am always asking myself and God what my heart and motive is any time I decide to share or unmask. I want to share things *only* if I know other people need to hear it. I want to live from a place of purity and authenticity in my words and in my actions.

After allowing God to do His full work in my life, I can now confidently step into the things He has called me to do. Without the weight of the things I was trying to hide. Without constantly feeling like I am not enough. Now I know who I am, and I can be all that I was called to be. Life unmasked is constantly being rooted in God's truth when the world wants me to believe its lies.

A life unmasked takes courage every day to share your weakness, but it has brought some of the most genuine relationships into my life. A life beyond the mask requires simplicity and consistent obedience to God's Word.

I wish I could tell you that the transformation of your identity and journey to wholeness will be a big, beautiful story with colorful rainbows and promises and burning bush moments. Looking back, I know that I am whole *not* because of all the BIG moments I had with God, but more so because of the consistency and commitment that I had to the process. The small, everyday decisions have made my roots grow deep. The days where I felt distant from God – but pursued Him anyways – have transformed my mind.

To unmask and live a life unmasked takes work. It takes the attitude of not giving up. Let me tell you, friends, there have been so many times on my journey where I simply wanted to give up. I knew if I could just go back to that girl who kept her junk in the closet, life would be safer.

It would protect me from this life of vulnerability that I knew God had called me to live out. But I just kept saying yes to God instead of yes to fear.

I hope you do, too, as God continues to work in your life one layer at a time. I pray you to find the courage to live out your story and truth. I hope that, through reading my journey, you have found yourself ready to use your pain and turn it into your purpose.

I hope that you find the courage to own your unfiltered life and that you wear it proudly. That you would find your true identity underneath the masks that have held you captive. I pray that you take the message of unmasking with you wherever you go. You never know whose life will be changed by hearing your story.

DISCUSSION QUESTIONS

hapter 1

What is the one thing about your story that you find the hardest to talk about?

What is the mask that you use to cover or hide hard things?

Do you feel the pressure to portray a "perfect" life?

hapter 2

How could you take better responsibility for your healing?

Have you truly forgiven the people who have hurt you?

Do you minimize your dreams because of your past?

Chapter 3
1. Do you remember your very first insecurity?
2. How have your insecurities changed over time?
3. What has your insecurity cost you?

Chapter 4
1. Name something you felt (or feel) rejected by.
2. In what ways do you cover your feelings of rejection?
3. Can you fully grasp that rejection is God's intervention?

Chapter 5
1. Have you ever felt unworthy because of something you felt ashamed of?
2. What can you think of that you may be hiding from God when He really wants to heal you?
3. Do you find yourself in the cycle of shame? What can you do to get yourself out?

Chapter 6
1. What are some things that make you fearful?
2. Would you consider yourself someone who must be in control?
3. Do you find yourself making a plan B? If so, why do you think you do this?

Chapter 7
1. Do you live a life of owning your story?
2. What does "owning your struggles" look like to you?
3. Do you practice James 5:16, confessing your struggles to someone you can trust for accountability, or do you find yourself too scared to unmask?

Chapter 8
1. What limits have you faced from not yet being completely healed?
2. Do you ask for help when you need it?
3. Can you think of something God healed you from that has made you better?

Chapter 9
1. Do you find yourself trying to protect your heart from feeling rejection?
2. How can you fight your battles through vulnerability?
3. How can you live a life of freedom from your past?

Chapter 10
1. Have you looked at your life more like a shattered glass or more like a puzzle piece?
2. What are some views you have about God that have been tainted by your personal story or upbringing?
3. Do you believe wholeness is a gift?

Chapter 11

1. What about the author's story most relates to your own story?
2. What are some practical ways you can walk out obedience?
3. Would you share your story if God asked you to?

Made in the USA
Columbia, SC
24 September 2020

21477338R00067